MAN-FATE

Also by William Everson

The Residual Years: Poems 1934–1948

William Everson, 1912-

MAN-FATE

The Swan Song of Brother Antoninus

A New Directions Book

ACKNOWLEDGMENTS
Acknowledgment is gratefully tendered the publishers and magazines
which previously issued parts of this book: Cayucos Books for "Tendril
in the Mesh"; The Lime Kiln Press for "Gale at Dawn"; Didymus Press
for "The Black Hills"; *Lemmings* for "Socket of Consequence"; *Sundaze*
for "Dark Waters"; and *The Maryland Poetry Review* for "The Man-
Fate," "Seed," "The Gauge," and "The Gash." "Tendril in the Mesh"
also appeared in *New Directions in Prose and Poetry 28*.

Manufactured in the United States of America
First published clothbound (ISBN: 0–8112–0520–7) and as New
Directions Paperbook 368 (ISBN: 0–8112–0521–5) in 1974
Published simultaneously in Canada by McClelland & Stewart, Ltd.

New Directions Books are published for James Laughlin
by New Directions Publishing Corporation,
333 Sixth Avenue, New York 10014

CONTENTS

IV. THE NARROWS

PREFACE

These are the poems of a man undergoing a major break fairly late in his years. It is a love poem sequence, a cycle of renewal, but it also concerns the monastic life, from the point of view of one who has renounced it. The love of woman and the love of solitude have contested together, and solitude has lost.

The first sequence, "Tendril in the Mesh," was written while the author was still in vows. Because it is the last piece in which he speaks from the persona of the monk it gives to the entire collection its defining subtitle: *The Swan Song of Brother Antoninus*. The swan, of course, is a phallic animal, and its associations are profoundly pagan. Zeus used it to deceive the simplicity of Leda, a myth testifying to the divine attribution in the archetype. Later culture, however, has injected an accent of irony into the term. The Swan Song is the last song, to be sure, the final performance, and inescapably lends itself to heavy pathos. But for the performer himself the implication is that he is finished without quite realizing it. He senses the moment is great, he feels he is still at the height of his powers, and perhaps he is, but only as he speaks does he become aware that his time is up.

"Tendril in the Mesh," done between 1966 and 1968, at Kentfield Priory in Marin County on San Francisco Bay, was composed when the author had no intention of leaving his Order. But by the end of 1969 the karma of his passion overwhelmed him, and in his final appearance as a monk, on the afternoon of December 7 at the University of California, Davis, he read the sequence publicly for the first time, as a monk making it his Swan Song indeed. Concluding his reading he stripped off his religious habit and fled the platform.

All the rest of the poetry is aftermath. At Stinson Beach, a small oceanside community north of San Francisco, he took up residence with his young wife Susanna, and her infant son. There he began to work out the implications of his break, composing across the years 1970 and 1971 the troubled verse that completes this volume.

In the fall of 1971 he became poet in residence of Kresge College, the University of California, Santa Cruz, and another phase of his life began. The irony is not lessened by the fact that the Santa Cruz Mountains district in which he found his home bears the name of his bird of nemesis. When, in the autumn of his arrival, he watched one of the great whistling swans, which winter in California, rise from his creekmouth lagoon, he thought of Jeffers's lines, and his own fate, and that of humankind:

Sad sons of the stormy fall,
No escape, you have to inflict and endure; surely it is time
* for you*
To learn to touch the diamond within to the diamond outside,
Thinning your humanity a little between the invulnerable
* diamonds,*
Knowing that your angry choices and hopes and terrors are
* in vain,*
But life and death not in vain; and the world is like a flight
* of swans.*

At Swanton new poems began to come, more objective, mercifully delivered from the excoriating introspection; but it has seemed best to confine this volume to the Stinson Beach poetry, retaining it as the contour of the break, another chronicle of division, karma reaping its inexorable fruit. A consecutive destiny clearly groups these poems together; but love of God is the thread that makes them one.

viii

How this book will be received by a public accustomed to hearing him speak as a monk the author cannot know, and he has hesitated long before submitting it. But he takes heart from the advice of a friend who observed, "Actually, the public has a better idea of where you are than ever before. When you spoke as a monk people were impressed, yet the monastery was really too remote for them to completely understand you. But to have lived a full life, renounced it for God, and then, almost two decades later, returned to the world, this is something everyone can respond to. It is time for you to publish. The public has sufficient media knowledge of your leaving the Order. Let the poetry give them the inner current."

Here, then, is that current, alternating between affirmation and denial, jubilation and guilt, in this author's characteristic (some would say interminable) wrestling with his soul. A recent anthologist has protested, "Antoninus' work composes not a spiritual odyssey, but an agony, a bitter quarrel with God." Actually, his only quarrel is with himself, and his odyssey goes on, no agony can impugn it. Certainly it cannot be served by ignoring realities. Those who counsel religious say it takes at least three years to emerge from the ordeal of renouncing vows. For the author, that interval has now been traversed, and he would never go back. But he cannot deny that too much of his heart lies there in his monastic cell for him to ever fully recover it.

WILLIAM EVERSON

October 20, 1973
Swanton, California

I
TENDRIL IN THE MESH

TENDRIL IN THE MESH

to Susanna

PROLOGUE

So the sea stands up to the shore, banging his chains,
Like a criminal beating his head on the slats of his cage,
Morosely shucking the onerous staves of his rage. And
    his custom
Of eyeing his plight, with malevolent fondness, never
    is done.
For he waits out the span of his sentence, but is undismayed;
He stands and expects, he attends
The rising up, the crest, the eventual slump of the sun.

For he bears in his groin his most precious jewel, the sacred
    fire of his crime,
Who pursued, like the beam of a laser, its solemn command,
Across the shires, red charts of his soul, the wrinkled map
    of his hand. And his heart,
Ridiculous, by someone denied, of a country preferment,
    never quits,
But clutches its need, like a duck. Somewhere his stain
Discolors the bride of defilement, whom rapine requested,
    under the form of his need, a ventral
Oath. But parched without peace, a swollen defeat, the
    cunning sleep of the slain.

Pluto, regnant occultist, lord of the lorns of lost space,
    the serene distances fringing the skirts of the night,
Gleaming back from his visor the farthest, most tentative
    beam of the light,
Whom Kore constrained, with her hesitant breast, above his
    drooping narcissist plant,
To twine in her arms his loud male thong, his truncheon
    desire, and the flex and thrill of his chant.

She was bud. Daughter of Zeus, the Father, whose need
    Pluto was,
Of the incestuous darkness the daughter provokes in the sire,
When she comes of the blood; when a menstrual spurt, astart,
    pulses out of her loin,
And she quivers her sleeks, and exclaims, and her mother
Nods and denies, and watches her wander, bait for the god,
Believing it well; though she frowns, she smiles and sighs.

So pitiful Pluto, occultist betrayed, by the quince
Of a maid ensorcelled, daughter of god, of himself unable,
    succumbed and was drawn,
From the cool of monastic deeps, the slats of his cage,
    where he beat his brains,
Where he knelt in prayer, and shook the chains of his vows,
And clawed his breast in a rage. Persephone smiles,
The pomegranate seed in her pouch, her jewel of rape, and
    the stain
Of his lust on her lip. She measures his term. Cringing,
He sleeps on unappeased, in the hush of the solemnly slain.

Now sigh the plight of all sires, who groan in their sleep,
When their daughter, divested, glides by in a dream,
Alight with a mauve desire, as of spring,
When barley is born to the year. O sing
Of all sires, whose passion, Plutonic, gnarls in the heart
In the immemorial fashion
Of fathers, and groan of the unspeakable thing.

4

But fight through to the forcing. And, gasping, pull back
    to see
In the dream if the hymen is crisped on the violent cod like
    a ring
Of her lips, torn flower, salt clung
Spoil of her triumph. But the aghast heart
Foretells in terror the shrink, the shy inexorable cower
Of the repulsed flesh. But an increase of need.
Oh my God the terrible torch of her power!

I

And it creams: from under her elbow a suffix of light,
    a sheen of kept being,
What the gleam from along her arm prefigures of quest.
I sense over slopes a rondure of presence invoked.
In the small of the girl, where hips greet the waist,
A redolence lurks in the crease, a rift of repose.

And I take in a long loop of arm everything seascapes
    prefigure of dusk:
Sycamore-sweeps, the tableaux of massed chaparral, a rouse
    of rowans.
Let sea-licked winds wrap the inch of their roots
    with evening
There to compose what the chewn leaves of the tan oak
    pucker up on the tongue;
And there, like a wand, wonderment's long awakening,
    strong shaftings of light.

No, never. Not one shall survive. When two such as we are
    outlaunched on desire, neither one comes back.
We have staked out our bodies on mesas of glimmering vetch.
We have mapped territorial claims on plateaus ripe for
    inclusion.
Sentinels spring up alarmed: the guardians of places remote
    are alerted to cover our foray.

Scalptakers, yes. And have waited out eons of stealth to
    stalk our quarry.
Now our needs converge; we join in a scuffle of perns.
The nets and the spears of beaters off there in the dark
    enflank us.
When the cry of the hunter broke over the flesh we fled
    them afar.
We emmeshed our bodies in thickets, entoiled in the brush.

I am old as the prairies and wise as the seams of worn
    granite, but she is new burgeoned.
New as the minted tin, as sleek as the calmness of ivory
    engravers have tooled for emblems.
A girl like the glide of an eel, like the flex of a serpent
    startled.
But I catch her in throes of pulsation; we are wantoned
    in groves.

Crotch and thigh; she is reft. Let me break white flesh
    asunder to cock this woman.
In the glimmer of night a wedge of fern configures her croft.
Maidenhair snuggles the cleft. Its shadow conceals and
    defines.
When I dip my lips to drink of that spring I throat the
    torrent of life.

For passion subsumes: what is focused is fixed, denotes its
    spang of vector.
A long supple swell of belly prescinds from extinction.
When I reach above for the breasts my arm is a laser
    unleashed.
I have knifed through dooms that spelt long since the death
    of man's spirit.

I have fastened my heart on the stitch of your voice, little
  wince of delight in the thicket,
Where the slim trout flick like a glint of tin in the
  pesky shallows.
Salacity keels; our itch of an ardent desire consumes and
  engorges my being.
I cannot look on your face; but my fingers start toward
  pockets of peace that lurk in your armpits.

Wild stallions of shuddering need squeal jumps of joy at
  your whistle.
I feel them snort in my ribs, they snuff for foods long
  bilked in their pleas for existence.
Now they snook and are all transfigured in sudden aerial
  manœuvres.
They skip like gnats in the shafts, made mad of your moan.

Give me your nipples to lip and your ribs to caress,
Take down from your shoulders the silks that have baffled
  the sun.
But retain as your own the cordage of menacing loves,
Those fingers of others before me that seethed and passioned,
Those hungers you held in the crimp of your flesh,
  confounding possession.

For I sense the pungence of death alert in your loins,
  little woman:
All men in the past who have lain on the wand of your body.
Your belly is seeded with sperm, the slick of lovers
  cinctures your waist like the wake of snails.
I cannot expunge from your flesh what they wrought, or
  annul their passion.

But do not withhold from my gaze what from everyone else
  you concealed:
The remotest part of your heart that you kept immured like
  a jewel.

7

When I touch it to see in your eyes the sheerest expansion
    of terror,
To taste on your stretched out tongue as you die the tensile
    nerve of its anguish,
I know I have fastened the nail, I have quicked your core
    of existence.

For I am the actual. Telluric forces are groined in my being.
Uranian urgencies coil of their strengths in my soul's
    narrow passes.
Out of my sinews deep starts of hunger yield mixed
    epiphanies:
The snake that sleeps in the stones and comes forth out
    of winter;
The great cat of the mountain that stalks for fawns in the
    darkening barrows.

I am the grizzly that grapples his mate in his hug of
    sheerest survival,
The salmon that jells his milt on the clutch his woman has
    sown in the gravel.
I am the river that breaks its back and pitches into the bay,
The osprey that jackknifes sidewise in surf to talon
    his quarry.

And I am the sea, its music, its instinct and whisper.
I encurl your rocks with my spill and embrace your shoulders.
In my estuary arms I entwine and enfold your thighs, I sleek
    your buttocks.
On my girth you toss like a chip to the crest of crude torrents.
When the great ships put out of port across my presence
Their seahorns chant me, sing mournful tones of presaging
    loss.

No ridge but the bone crest of power in the continent's nape.
A glaze of light is riddling the sheen of the wheat of Tehema.
Have the winds of Point Reyes, festooned with spindrift,
    declared anything other?
Do they glare for the spoil of the sun? Do they ache for
    the couches of night?

No bridge avails but the stretched out flesh of its coupling
    hunger.
Between the split of your thighs I plant spurts of voracious
    pleasure.
Not a hair of the nock that a woman widens anent the cob
    resists of a love.
On the nodes of transparent worlds we collapse, we pant
    and expire.

In all darks is my joy defined, that plaza, those nubian
    porches,
There my whole tongue turns in the col of your beating body.
In my hands of a man the sense is awake to mold idols of
    flesh for victims.
Plunged to the wrists I feel passion spurt through the
    instincts meshed in your nerves,
The peaks of clitoral quickness jetting spunk in a viscid issue.

You come back to be coaxed: I have caught you between the
    cheeks and will never be stinted.
Entwined in your thirst I tangle hair, the riatas of
    your desire.
In order to crest I snake angles of coupled completeness.
A flinch of fire, something struck. from the meshes of passion,
    clusters my neck.

Do not think to be stronger than death; to die is to drink desire.
To die is to take at the pitch of madness one fabled stroke
    of disinterest.

9

I have felt on those fields the light that a passion decreed,
    spined on sheer splendor.
When you moan and expire shrewd arrows of truth, shot
    through shields of zinc, pierce my belly.

Now I ken where suns have gone down when they quitted
    our country.
It is not as if they had nothing to gain in defaulting.
Rather with us for cause they seek stratas, new zones
    of extinction.
They annihilate zeros, total steeps to expunge; like us,
    they erase their condition.

Now my fingers conclude. They have founded whole sweeps
    of existence,
Have soaked up splendor in jets, have fed to the final.
No trace remains of what was; across the line of my life
Your breast pounds and proves; the sound of your heart
    extols its ancient surrender.

II

Man of God. Tall man, man of oath. Mad man of ignorant
    causes.
Like the mast of a ship, like the weathered spar of
    a schooner.
Long shank of a man, whose hair is all whetted with frost,
    and a nick of silver.
What inch of enactment cinctured your loins and is freed?
I can feel in my knees the scruff of time's thrust as you
    take me.

Finger of God! A stipple of terror shudders my skin when
    you touch me!
Who are you? In your eyes is the passion of John the Baptist
    and the folly of Christ!

10

Do not drop me! I have never been known of man, really,
   before you possessed me!
By all men, of any, who have bruised and straightened
   my body,
The marks of their hands are erased of your lips. I never
   knew them!

Now teach me your deeps! Prophet and utterer of godly
   imponderable oaths, great prayers of anguish.
Guru of my bed, who have taught me koans of revealment.
Adept of niches and slots, my woman's being convulses in
   truth for your entry!
When your hands work marvels I fear I will die, will faint
   in your swells of compression.

Let rivers that run to the sea be my attestation.
You took me on Tamalpais, in the leaf, under Steep Ravine
   redwoods.
The bark of trees was broken to tear and divest me.
On the brow of the hill that brinks its base you thrusted
   me up to your God.

Beast and Christian! What manner of dog do you worship for
   Christ that you must rend and devour!
I have felt in my womb the index of Him you call God.
Do you wasten life that my flesh and my bone should be
   wholly consumed of your spirit?
What is His face if the eyes you blaze are the tusks
   of carnivores?

I have no defenses against your truth and desire none.
Make me a Christian, then do what you want with this dross,
For a strange pale fury that cannot be natural consumes me.
I blink back tears of relief to feel in your hands the awe
   of Him you adore.
Is your vow of a monk meant to serve for the seal of
   your lust?

For your lust of a monk is a hunger of all God's seekers.
In my nerve's raw marrow I feel Him teach me His witness.
Let me go! But do not desert what you chose to instruct.
If I cannot reckon what unstrings my knees what worth
    is survival?

Let me go! No, but breach my belly with godly unspeakable
    anguish!
This split of thighs you desire is more than my means.
Your face is flensed with an awesome devouring passion.
In the flukes of contortion I fear what I see as I need it.
My body is written with poems your fingers enscrolled on
    my flesh.

Let no woman survive me, old man, mad man of the mountain,
Wily old buck of the benches and bull elk of somnolent mesas.
Monk of the seashore and friar of granite enclosures,
The mad holy man who spread my legs for entry.
As the crotch of cloistered enclosures my flesh is empaled
    on your spirit!

III

And the storm swings in from the sea with a smashing
    of floats.
There are hulks on the rocks where wrecks broke splintering
    up under waves.
A kindling-making wind is tearing out scrub on the jaw of
    the hill,
And the encompassed bay where fishermen loafed is found a
    cauldron of spume.

Let it blow! Now a wild rejoicing of heart springs up
    in answer!
After summer's stultification what more can penetrate
    deadness?

The nerves that have slept for so long in the simmering
   flesh, complacent with languor,
Awaken to swing their stutter of fright at the crash
   of billows.

And those casual loves are swept out. Only a troth as stark
   as the tooth,
Elemental and sheer as the hurricane's whetstone incisor;
Only a love as crunched as the jaw of the cougar,
When the passion-responders grope for each other under the
   pelt of the storm.

They will find in the rain what can match the spatter of
   hail on a house.
They will know where to slake when the trees break free of
   what heaps at their knees.

And they moan. Couched on beach grass under shelter of drift
They hug each other. They watch with the zeal of love the
   hurricane's howl.
With one eye bent to the weather they see the light on the
   head at Point Reyes
Hum like an axhead held to the stone, the sparks a spurt
   shooting leeward.

Now crawl to me shivering with love and dripping with rain,
Crawl into my arms and smother my mouth with wet kisses.
Like a little green frog slit the cleft of your thighs
   athwart me.
The rain on your face is the seed of the stallion strewn as
   it spits blue fire.

For the lightning forks like one naked the seething thud of
   the sea.
And swells like a woman's in birth when she heaves up
   her belly.

She has braced her heels on the land; her beaches are
    benched to that passion,
And her crotch is the hollow, sunk low under wind-heap
    waves, when its back breaks over.

She is fouled of bad weather but never of love, this woman.
In her blood the groan and travail of a birth is being
    fashioned.
Her spilth like the gasp of stallions clings round her ankles.
And her vulva tilts thwart the wind's wide lip when he
    whistles his force through her body.

Now crawl to me under this driftwood hutch and cower
    upon me.
Warm the stitch of rain in the drench of passion and forget
    to be frightened.
But build in your womb's young realm the germ of your
    mother the sea.
For to be found in this labor sunk under a shelf she was
    nothing loath of her mating.

Oh splendor of storm and breathing! O woman! O voice
    of desire!
Tall power of terminal heights where the rain-whitened peaks
    glisten wet!
But the heave of slow-falling sleep will follow outpouring
    in winter's wake.
This too is your meed when passion is flashed for blood in
    the typhoon's crater.

Now sleep in my arms, little newt, little mite of the water,
Little wind-beaten frog, pale delicate limper alone on
    sea-pulled pebbles.
Go to sleep and awaken in spring when your blood requickens.
And bear back to man in your flesh the subtle sign of him
    who marked you for God.

IV

Daughter of earth and child of the wave be appeased,
Who have granted fulfillment and fed the flesh in the spirit.
A murmur of memory, a feint of infrequent espousals,
And the tug of repose the heart hovers and tilts toward dawn.

Somewhere your body relinquishes creeds of defiance.
I have tasted salt salience, and savored its fragrance, have
    crested repose.
Now appeasement crouches and wends its way through my
    being.
I sense fulfillment not breached of strings and torches.

Kore! Daughter of dawn! Persephone! Maiden of twilight!
Sucked down into Pluto's unsearchable night for your husband.
I see you depart, bearing the pomegranate seed in your groin.
In the node of your flesh you drip my flake of bestowal.

What will you do, back on earth, when you find your mother?
Will the trace of dark lips fade out of your flesh forever?
I have knocked your instep with rapture, I have wounded
    your flank.
Like the little fish in the dredger's boat you bear the teeth
    of the gaff.

O daughter of God! When the sons of man covet your passion,
Do not forget who placed on your brow his scarab of
    sovereign possession.
In the service of holy desire bear truth for escutcheon.
And when you return to the roost of night wear the mane of
    the sun!

Dark God of Eros, Christ of the buried brood,
Stone-channeled beast of ecstasy and fire,
The angelic wisdom in the serpentine desire,
Fang hidden in the flesh's velvet hood
Riddling with delight its visionary good.

Dark God of Eros, Christ of the inching beam,
Groping toward midnight in a flinch of birth,
The mystic properties of womb and earth:
Conceived in semblance of a fiercer dream,
Scorning the instances of things that merely seem.

Torch of the sensual tinder, cry of mind,
A thirst for surcease and a pang of joy,
The power coiled beneath the spirit's cloy,
A current buckling through the sunken mind,
A dark descent inventive of a god gone blind.

The rash of childhood and the purl of youth
Batten on phantoms that once gulled the soul,
Nor contravened the glibness in the role.
But the goad of God pursues, the relentless tooth
Thrills through the bone the objurgation of its truth.

Often the senses trace that simmering sound,
As one, ear pressed to earth, detects the tone
Midway between a whisper and a moan,
That madness makes when its true mode is found,
And all its incremental chaos runs to ground.

Hoarse in the seam of granite groans the oak,
Cold in the vein of basalt whines the seed,
Indemnify the instinct in the need.
The force that stuttered till the stone awoke
Compounds its fluent power, shudders the sudden stroke.

Dark Eros of the soul, Christ of the startled flesh,
Drill through my veins and strengthen me to feed
On the red rapture of thy tongueless need.
Evince in me the tendril in the mesh,
The faultless nerve that quickens paradise afresh.

Call to me Christ, sound in my twittering blood,
Nor suffer me to scamp what I should know
Of the being's unsubduable will to grow.
Do thou invest the passion in the flood
And keep inviolate what thou created good!

II
RITE OF PASSAGE

EBB AT EVENING

Tide-turn: and the surf
Swept back from the shore,
Crouched shuddering on its flat mat,
Unable to rise.

When the tide
Hunkers low like this on squat hams
Everything bates breath.

It is the solstice, the hip of the year
Bent double, the body of earth
Clenched for passage, time's
Ancient art, the deep
Rite of renewal.

In the evening ebb, as the sun
Wallows under a skirt of cloud and flares low,
Many people come forth to traverse the beach,
Seeking shells, stones, strange fragments of drift,
Seed of the lost fecundity
Borne back to their lives.

Now the sun is gone.

But the cloud
Defers, sidling offshore. For a moment
The beach, in the oblique
Bifurcation of dusk, confronts the west,
Immense and abstract, a massive slab.

The neap tide turns.

And the dark
Drops.

     And the sea,
An awakening woman,
Simultaneously rising and turning, impulse
Groined in the ripple of immense repose,
The sea
Stands up in her bed and stares.

THE MAN-FATE

Susanna: girl and bride,
You sleep in the adjoining room,
And I sense the sea, at solstice,
Tide-turn, pivot and close in.

This turning of my life,
Like the long withdrawing wave,
Checks, wheels, steps forward.

And what was sucking fast underfoot,
The rustle of sea-pulled pebbles,
Swings back and resurges.

The fate of man
Turns on the body of woman.
She takes the long advance
And the long recession.
By what she is
She defines them.

In the dusk,
In the adjacent room,
I hear your body
Stir in its berth.

The moan you make
Is a murmur of seabirds.
It marks the turning of the day.

The tide turns.
The season turns.
The year turns.

And life
Curls on the node of its solemn disclosure,
And gropes renewal.

SEED

Some seed in me,
Some troublous birth,
Like an awkward awakening,
Stirs into life.

Terrible and instinctive
It touches my guts.

I fear and resist it,
Crouch down on my norms, a man's
Patent assurances.

I do not know its nature.
I have no term for it.
I cannot see its shape.

But there, inscrutable,
Just underground,
Is the long-avoided latency.

Like the mushrooms in the oakwood,
Where the high-sloped mountain
Benches the sea,

When the faint rains of November
Damp down the duff,
Wakening their spores—

Like them,
Gross, thick and compelling,
What I fear and desire
Pokes up its head.

THE GAUGE

Time is the gauger of all things,
And the solver of all things.

Wrapped in its breast
The nature of consequence
Peaks and divulges.

Only in consequence
Is implication verified.

Only in time
Is implication, consequence,
Actualized.

In my span of existence
I touch with new hands
Its wake of passage.

Out of its belly,
Time's opulent womb,
The nature of the actual
Quickens, is born.

Susanna, I hear your body
Turn in the dusk; the great
Languor of life
Broods on the shadowy lids of your eyes,
Where you sigh,
Where you sleep.

Howler of gulfs and sunken undredgable deeps,
Time flows, curls over your body, as a wave
Cups stone on the bench of this sea,
And restores me, the God-blunted man,
To my measure.

SOCKET OF CONSEQUENCE

On Stinson Beach, long spit of sand scything the sea,
A clutter of beach homes and summer cottages
Sprawls beneath the wind's pelt.
A few shore pines and cypresses protect from the gales
The love nests, the hippy pads and the homosexual lairs.
And we, among them and of them,
A fugitive monk and an unwed mother,
Making love in the solstice weather,
Thread time's needle eye,
Clasp in a welter of conclusive rapture.
Blow out of the Pacific,
The vast waters beyond the Farralones,
O wind of the solstice and the knuckle of the year.
Within your arms I embrace the twin facts of love and death:
Death of the past, the love
Of future and the life, one rapture that abides.
Under us the perdurable sand,
That shifts and washes and remains forever,
Gift of the sea, gift of the wind's
Somber indirection, and the vane of time,
Changing, changing on its hub,
Spelling out of the socket of consequence
Its terror and its truth.

THE GASH

To covet and resist for years, and then
To succumb, is a fearsome thing. All you craved and denied
At last possesses you. You give yourself
Wholly to its power; and its presence,
Invading your soul, stupefies
With its solace and its terror.

There is nothing so humbling as acceptance.

I sense the mushrooms in the night,
Tearing their way up through loose soil,
Brutal as all birth.

                And I bend my head,
And cup my mouth on the gash of everything I craved,
And am ravaged with joy.

GALE AT DAWN

Landwind: a gale at dawn scooping down from the hills.
It pours west to the water, hits the foam
Like a counterattack repulsing a beach landing.

But the brute surf stalks in, stupendous breakers
Born out at sea, inexorably arriving.

The landwind, honing them, combs back their furls,
And the low winter light, shining flatly through,
Wreathes the powerful, doomed shoulders,
Gives each lion wave its rainbow mane,
Hackled with gold.

              But the wind,
Like a holy terror, rips back those brows.
Plunged in the hollow of each ponderous breast
It explodes into fire.

O wind and water! Like a gale at dawn
Man hits the wave of woman. She arches her throat
For the stab of his lips. Over the wallowing blood
His sudden face divides her life; his terrible gift
Wreathes her with flame.

           At dusk
All falls still. The air, curiously spent,
Hangs inert.

           We savor salt.

                In the immense quietude,
Under the nimbus of sunset, we find by the water
The surf-quenched scoter, the depth-disheveled grebe.

III
A TIME TO MOURN

A TIME TO MOURN

A time to weep, and a time to laugh.
A time to mourn, and a time to dance.
ECCLESIASTES

A time to mourn.

For to suffer the loss of a way of life
Is as hard a hurt
As the loss of the closest friend.

A time to grieve.

For when the fates
Exact, drive home their denial,
A great hole is left in the breast,
A gap and a gulf,
Where all that was once most meaningful
Is ripped away.

Grieve, then, and not grudge the grieving.
Mourn without shame.
For what life asserts
The self must swallow.
On its own dark curd
The soul must suck.

Though a man in his going
Be filled with delight,
The leap of liberation—

31

His hurt of avowal,
Of broken allegiance,
Is not to be scanted.

Truly, the loss of a primal way of life
Is like the going of a great love.

One carries it within,
A festering sorrow,
An unfillable lack.

And the delicate
Feeder-roots of the soul,
Denied their sustenance,
Starve and shrink back.

So the sea falls, falls.
The tides return.
The long apostleship of the surf,
Revolving over and over,
Shapes its harsh indenture.

Obscuring as much as it clarifies,
It fills its function,
Effects what it denotes.

And once again, in the ineffable
Gulf of alienation,
On Stinson Beach I ponder fate.

I grope the impacted nucleus,
The paradox of love and denial,
My taproot of guilt.

And the fresh wind,
Obliquely out of the south,
A breath of charge and renewal,
Cross-angles my brow.

I lift up my face.
On the far horizon
One flake of sail
Skitters and dips.

Then my sight drops.
When my gaze levels,
Steep surf accosts it.

*

Offshore, swimming leisurely south,
A pride of sea lions
Glimpses me first.

Instantly alert
They lift their shoulders
Stiffly from the surge,
Gazing intently landward, fixing me
Where I stand, the one
Conspicuous object on the beach.

Curious and suspicious
They float warily with the drift,
Hieratic and immobile as tritons,
Lords of the sovereign sea.

Their august presence
Accuses me. At one with their element,
Knowing no remorse, they are what they are.

I am what I am not.

And the span of my attention
Snaps back, coddles my grief.
I envy them, with a wild throttling yearn,
Their serene composure, their calm
Simplicity of being.

*

In the monastic life
Celibacy is the catalyst of fire,
The signature of the ultimate.

It is the cross upon which the monk
Crucifies his intuition
In the spasm of God's grace: desire
Memorialized in the rapture of the spirit.

Out of the clench of the flesh, its energies
Transform instinct into awareness,
The octave of comprehension.

In the seal of its assurance
A man invokes encounter, the impenetrable
Gaze of God.

Who knows it
Knows the power of banked fire,
Outlasting the thirst of life,
A sentient flare.

*

Westward the surf falls,
Somberly and without cessation,
On the pulse-stroke of man's blood,
Revamping under our feet
The fundamental berm, this beach, our narrow
Shelf of existence.

The sea lions are gone. In their place,
Beyond the white line of the breakers,
Drifts a gaggle of surfers, oblique on their boards,
Facing seaward.

　　　　　From the shore
One sees but the tilted torsos,
Tense shoulders, the alert heads.
They look to the far
Wrinkling of the sea, surmising increment:
Which influx of the swell, impending,
Will coalesce into consequentiality,
Engender thrust, and, reaching forward,
Stoop towering in, all ultimate
Augmentation.

　　　　　This, in their mind's eye,
Is the vision of beatitude:
The great wave of their wonder.

Like the paired sea lions,
Equally alert, equally sustained,
They float immobile, awaiting their instant.
But where the sea lions, water creatures,
Looked in to the shore,
These drifters, essentially land animals,
Gaze narrowly out to sea.

So do the divisible natures of life
Look to otherness for significance.
And just so does the heart,
An organ of the blood, look to the spirit.
Only then can it find its singular definition,
Its rare essential meaning.

A strange breed, surfers of the salt.
Neither landsmen nor sailors,
Neither flyers nor divers,
They inhabit the obscure interval,
The zone of force and chaos,
(Force of the swell, chaos of the cracking wave)
That obtains between the primary entities,
The worlds of earth and water.

Awaiting the momentary surge, the eluctable thrust,
Each will turn tail, seize
Groundswell in its strong inception, climb
The shark-shape board, pick
Power from the heave, to come shearing in,
Utterly at ease under the arched
Immensity of the wave.

Then, in the final deft manœuver,
When the breaker is quelled, its force
Spent, its momentum
Gone—then,
Redisposing body weight on the tipped feet,
The surfer deflects, blades sideways,
Climbs the inside of the wave's depleted convexity,
Pauses balanced along the purling subdued crest,
And, the long surf's power abandoned to the shore,
Drops lightly down, crests the tilting board,
And prows it back to sea.

I watch them,
And I watch the wave,
The unity of force and response,
The ease of conjoined purposes.

A time to mourn.
A time to savor hurt.
A time to turn the mind's blade
Back on the heart,
The pierce of self-recognition.

And let the living gaze
Gouge to the guts.

*

The monastic life as well
Absorbs the surge-point of the real,
The interlude of force and chaos
Between God and the soul.
(Groundswell of events,
Chaos of the cracking world.)
And like the surfer,
Silently intent and electrically alert,
The monk, too, watches the shape of things,
The riptide of events,
For the ingathering flux.
Mounting it, he seizes power, the world's
Hidden transtemporal force,
The wave of the future.
This he takes, takes it at the pitch,
The steep insurge of investing time,
Climbs, crests;
Then, spent of his instancy,
He yields to the deep depletion,
And comes gliding in.

One of the great ways of life.
One of the primal vocations.
He who accepts it and betrays it
Spalls his integrity,
Insults his God.

And the sea affirms it,
Tell it as so, as true.

Utterly without equivocation
It speaks of certitude and denial.

Ever-changing, it has never forsworn its role.
Invincibly active, it has never ceased
Balancing the margin of victory
Between what abides and what alters. It allows
Every recourse, every omnidiversion,
Except the betrayal of essence.
And what essence is
Constitutes the nature,
Denotes the real.

A monk is a monk is a monk is a . . .

Given his commitment,
Whatever else proffers,
Be it never so evocative,
Is unthinkable, a thing
Not to be countenanced.

*

Over my head a shadowy intrusion,
A ripple of gulls, ringbills,
Larus delawarensis, float lightly in the air.

They ride the ripples
As the sea lions balance the groundswell,
As the surfers teeter the wave.

One and by one they glide over me,
Veering right and left as they go forward,
Each tilting the black-tipped beak of its insignia,
Its categorical distinction,
As if consciously authenticating its identity,
The manifest sign of presence:
That which confirms it.

It is what it is.

No, the habit does not make the monk,
No more than the ringed bill makes the gull.
But as positive distinctions
Each sign is intrinsic.
Each signifies an actuality,
True marks of the self.

Suddenly I see myself as nondescript,
Rootless and unbelonging, a fugitive identity:
Monk without monastery,
A friar without vows.

And the sea falls, falls.
The vast world of water
Lips the shore.
Southward, where the cliffs kneel,
It gnaws the rock bone of its mutable contention,
Growling and mouthing its sputum of intent.

And I nod to it, bending into it,
Half piqued with its sullen recalcitrance,
Unable to isolate, nor effectively categorize,
Save in the pit of my own subjectivity,
My rancor with my self.

A time to mourn and not contend.
A time to grieve and not be ashamed.
A time to moan, and accept consolation.

For the sea consoles.
In his time of need let that consolation
Be no man's scorn.

*

Suddenly by beach grass fringing the dunes
A flitter bats my eye. Black shape,
Skewed presence, a bandy-legged crow
Hop awkwardly, peering for fish heads,
Gills, fins, the scooped-out hulls of crustaceans,
Anything under the sun.

He caws me, derisive and unflappable.
Here on the beach, a creature utterly out of his element
But equally unrepentant,
Ineptly competing with gulls, sanderlings,
Phalaropes and willets, the diligent
Researchers of the shore,
For the surf's refuse, the offscouring sea,
He perks and skitters.
I skim a rock at him; he takes off, squawking.
Teetering on a twig he beaks the troughing wind
And scolds me. He blusters my head with his curse.

Whoever forsakes his element
Is ludicrous, and in his perverse
Exacerbation, damns his own eyes.

Or so I surmise.

*

Man has free will, no denying that; but freedom's
Accessibility to the soul
Is gauged on the apex of individual consciousness
Achieved in the man—a consciousness
All the fluent force of heredity,
Compressed in the resistant frame of environment,
Has basically contrived.

A consciousness
Subsumed in the ever-evolving awareness of the breed,
Wherein the great interior archetypes
Work their awesome way,
Grope toward clarification,
Painfully contesting dominion
In the hegemony of the soul,
The precise point in the blood's evolution
A man represents.

Man has free will, certainly.
But a will subsumed in the brute
Stubbornness of the earth, a stubbornness
Fluid but inflexible, the short seasons
Shaping him. Who can measure the hemispheric stress,
The stone-paced impress of geologic flux?
Or what the rock-beds of continents
Do to man's soul?

And islands?
Dappling the wine-dark sea
They redispose the elements,
Shaping anew our insular fates,
The singular destinies of all who inhabit them,
To make of old races
The tongues of new breeds.

I have soared, and seen beneath me
The flat plain of the Mississippi,
Apparently the absolute of levelness, but actually
All watershed, from the snow-pitched Rockies
To the Allegheny scarp,
Vaster than the aching eyes, contesting distance,
Can ever encompass. And have seen in its trough
The River itself, snake-nested,
Torpid in twilight, thick serpentine silver,
Uncoiling down the stretched
Alluvial plain, clean to the Gulf,
To bury its head, all unslaked thirst,
Deep in the uterine sea. On its curl
Whole cities deploy, and new peoples
Body forth substance in its sinuous girth.
My own mother shaped to its impress,
A child of those prairies,
And my father, in the Twin Cities astride it,
Endured transformation
From the stark Norwegian temper,
To the straight American cast. The very
Latitudes of the globe, so evocative in the mind,
Modify inheritance. Our eaten food
Determines our flesh. The trajectory
Of growth and decline as the sun charts it
Etches the red jag of its glyph
On the graph of our soul.
And when it relinquishes us into our fate
Our names change.

*

Man has free will, assuredly.
But the will of the world
Is subsumed in the will of the cyclic cosmos,

42

Where the planets, like floats on a maelstrom,
Mark the recurrence of galactic flux,
Each a creation of the complex of energies
Sustaining the universe: "The conversion
Of energy into mass." But the energy there
Before the mass, each star, each
Planet, a crest, a peaking
Of the operative complex,
Where the converging energy-fields transect,
As the presence of man, the individual human being, denotes
A corresponding peak of the same focus,
So that the energies peaking in the one
Conform to the energies peaking in the other,
The root energies, as it were, endowed there,
The planet nothing in itself, a sign,
As the man is a sign,
To be interpreted, yes, but attributed, never;
To be read, yes, but reverenced
Not at all.

      For man's free will
Like the cold will of earth,
Like the hot will of the cosmos,
Is subsumed in the inscrutable,
The savagely oblique will of God,
Shone through the great orchestration of the All,
His actuality of pure existence
Throbbing throughout the galactic spawn.
The solar system fluxes His force
Down through the ambient climate of earth
To the brute soul of evolving man,
Blind, split by temptation and crippled by sloth,
To touch the archetypes asleep there,
Each latent symbolic core,
Ordain his fierce evolution,
 The growth through pain and contradiction

To the point of unbearable consciousness,
The ego anguished between contesting powers,
The archetypal configuration within
And the planetary configuration without,
And all ordained. In the will of God
Subsumes the will of cosmos and earth.
In the will of God
Subsumes the pitiful will of man.

A time to mourn. A time to drink
Deep of the life-purge.
A time to slake pain
In the instance of acceptance.
To acknowledge and repent.

*

Last night, under the sudden
Solstice dusk, I left for a moment the crackling hearth.
I walked through sere beach grass
Gazing at stars.
Wrapped in the muffled night chill of earth
I stared at great Saturn,
A cold core glinting the East.
Gazing out of the burgeoning archetype
His place there denotes, I watched him, watched
Till the sinking rim shook him free,
As birth, the wild unfolding womb,
Frees what we are into what we will be.

For in the year of my birth
Saturn stood early in Gemini,
Sign of Communication, the first decan. On that instant
He swung through the Ninth House,
Not for nothing called the House of Religion.

Nor is it all for nothing
I was born to the vocation of religious poet.

And the planets that morning
Strung up the East like an express train,
From Uranus in the Fifth, the House of Creativity,
To culminating Saturn, the hard diamond of the cutting edge
Ploughing the sky. The horoscope
Charts the sequence. The open trine
Embraces the West, spans the sinking Descendant,
A configuration, in the literature of gestalt astrology,
Sometimes called the Locomotive Type.
As such it denotes a congenital force,
"A self-driving individuality, an executive
Eccentricity that is not queerness or unbalance
But rather is power." As leading planet,
Saturn decrees the point-focus of symbolic force.
For me, in the deeps of the endowed imagination,
Father and God are one. And they are terrible.

When I deny such presences,
When I controvert such determinants,
I violate my soul.

*

And I do deny them.

For in the First House, the House of Life,
Venus and Mars, conjunct on the same degree,
Clasp in a spasm of convulsive rapture.
Like Antony and Cleopatra
They exult in each other's arms,
Throwing whole empires away.
In Libra, Venus is paramount.

Mars, in his fall there, wallows into her womb,
Pouring his resplendent phallic strength
Between the grope of her clutching thighs.
All his sublimely militant energy,
Made to serve God as the sword serves the spirit,
Subverted from rooting out error
To rooting in the bed.

Like Samson shorn of his radiant locks,
Mars in Libra can prosper and excel
Only in the service of Venus.

                    She rules him!
She rules him!

           Let Saturn the Father
Intone from the pulpit his somber decrees,
But the power of procreation,
Flaming from the House of Life,
Defies proscription.

For eighteen years as a Dominican monk
Saturn, which rules my soul, reigned in my life.
Then Uranus, smasher of limits, moved into Libra,
The hammer of the thunderer jarred the scales,
Skewed the balance. In the arms of Mars,
With Uranus for goad,
Venus laughs at law.
High in the Ninth,
The House of Religion,
Mighty Saturn bows.

And the monk, gone crazy,
Flies his cell,
Forsakes his holy vows.

It is the disconsolate
Irony of life. And not even rare.
These are the episodes
Our tabloids daily flaunt: MAGISTRATE
FLIPS WITH B GIRL! STRIPPER
TAGS PROF! Should the monk, then,
In high disdain, account himself
Superior to these? Poor human facts
The world well knows, its genial code allows?
But if not, if he holds himself no higher,
Why, then, his vows?

And the sea falls,
Falls. Its sigh, the long whisper of mortality,
The syllable of consummation,
Pensive with understanding.

A time to mourn.
To drink deep of the sorrow of the life purge.
To slake the pain in the instance of avowal.
To acknowledge and repent.

*

I lift up my head.
The surfers are gone with the sea lions.
The gulls and the crow are no more.
Only the sea obtains,
Champing and gesticulating,
Throwing up the substance of its implication,
The reckoning spume,
Bestowing the salt of its wisdom
On the beaches of man's world.
Immemorially responsive,
Supremely acknowledging and participating,
The sea, in its endlessness, consoles.

When the selves within a man,
Like the sources in the cosmos,
Contest together,
What word denotes betrayal?

It is the heart that knows,
And it is the heart which whispers:

"God gives man freedom:
The power to do what he ought."

I chose.
Because I betrayed my vows.
I betrayed myself.

Because I betrayed myself
I have betrayed my God.

And the heart howks it up,
The old immemorial utterance,
The keyword of repentance:

"My fault, my fault, my most grievous fault!"

And the sea, like a mother,
Broods and reflects.
Within her vast attentive ear
My words, like offshore leaves,
Whirl out and sink down.
They settle in the surf.

And the surf responds,
Rippling and flowing,
The eternal flux,
The sublime benediction,
The whisper of silence.

Under the whisper
The stillness of the heart;
Under the crash of events,
Breaking, breaking—

But the heart,
Sounded on silence,
In quietude subsumes.

And absolution?

O my God! What have I forsaken?

Old sea, old mother,
Grant me surcease!

Lave my wounds
And lift me home!

IV
THE NARROWS

STORM AT LOW TIDE

A storm at low tide is like the dark night of the soul.
All the surface surge comes shattering in,
Impelled by a sixty-mile-an-hour gale
And something violent far out to sea
Menacing more. But the outgoing suck
Is relentless, and will not yield.
Caught between wind and moon
The water stands up to the beach going every which way
But perpendicularly contained in the inexorable tension,
A quivering wall poised to plunge,
And frighteningly twitching its skin like a demented horse,
Only to topple and collapse as if something utterly trivial
    had tripped it,
Scattering its myriad particles and fragments
In the ultimate exasperation of purposeless dispersion.
I walk along the tortured ribbon of foam that traces the
    violent nadir,
Reflecting how I too was torn so, knowing this rage
    of resistance,
This exasperate, desperate madness, this inexpressible
Chaotic lust.

THE NARROWS OF BIRTH

Christmas night: the solstice storm
Muttering in retreat, threatening rain,
Cypress witlessly clawing the roof,
Its vague hand scrawling the obscure
Prophecy of reprisal. Across the dunes
Wind rakes the hollow-breasted sea,
Coughing and expectorating like a consumptive invalid,
A feverish old woman racked in senility's
Festering decrepitude, morbidly ailing.

I awake from a dream of ritual slaying: beachfire
Back from the surf; hunched in an angle of logs and
    driftwood
Crouches the clan. Among them,
Free and unsuspecting, a youth lounges,
Perfectly relaxed, a man
Stalwart, high-minded and virile,
In the deceptive way the dream
Inveterately falsifies reality,
Approximating the ideal.
To me, in the freezing awareness of apprehension,
It becomes increasingly apparent
He is not to be their guest but their victim.
Yet my very prescience, which declares my involvement,
Renders me powerless. For I have entered into complicity,
A kind of unspoken pact, with these people,
    seeking something
They have which I need, which I once knew and lost,
And have come to recover in my own quest;
And because of this need, this involvement,
Have forfeited my freedom.

And suddenly, with great clarity of vision,
I see them for what they are,
The castrate sons and the runt daughters,
Maimed progeny of the Mother,
From whose destiny I myself, long ago, had somehow
    escaped,
And have returned now, improvidently,
To verify my lack. They hobble about their appointed tasks,
Preparing the terrible rites of immolation.
They seem to be concocting some kind of revolting brew,
The narcotic that renders the victim senseless,
Of which the elements, I am aware, are parlous:
Milk and dung, blood and semen, menses and afterbirth,
The mordant ingredients of parturition.
These, I see, stand for the universal postulates
    of generation:
Twin compulsions of Desire and Death:
The inexorable forces which every major religion
Has pitted itself to overcome; and from which
The vows of every monk
Are structured toward deliverance.

And I sense, from the depths of this recognition,
The utter ineffectuality of everything I am—my own
    monk's vows
Jettisoned in a spasm of precipitate repudiation,
Leaving me weaponless, hands utterly empty,
To grope my way back to these somnambulists,
These ominous dark sources,
In the reassessment of my life.

Across the fire I face the matriarch,
My ancient ancestress, the fountainhead of my blood,
Saying, "I have come back, Mother,"
And I bow my head as a penitent
Bows for absolution; or as the prodigal,

Having squandered his heritage,
Lowers his neck to signify his wrong.
But in the old mother of glittering eyes
Is neither absolution nor forgiveness.
Her gaze searches me narrowly,
Unrelenting, utterly unimpressed
By anything I might say,
Waiting for proof. She will be appeased now
Only by deeds—by words
Never.

       I waver in the firelight,
Uncertainly, unable to know
What it is I am to do, unable to reassert
Who I am, or say what brought me here,
What motive or what reasons avail
In this weirdly familiar place.

The plotting goes on.
I see the body of the youth,
Beautifully muscled, like Michelangelo's
Immortal slave, the raised shirt
Banded about the nipples,
And all the magnificent body
Slumped in its unmistakably erotic swoon.

The castration begins.

I wake to the dawn, bolt upright,
With the retreating storm
Muttering in the eaves, uncertain
And vague and foreboding.
I feel beside me in the strange bed
The body of my young wife.
She is breathing deeply in sleep,

The clear pulse of her being
Mustering within it all the life-force
Against my fear. In the next room
Her nine month's son cries out, softly,
Under the wince of my pervasive torment,
An anguish which haunts the house,
My pain and my guilt.
In the stretched silence
I touch her again, the flank of woman,
Modulant with the subsumed
Rapture of life. And everything I have come for
Clutches my throat,
Warring in the narrows of this birth.

THE CHALLENGE

Then what do I seek?
Truly, I know not.

                    Destiny,
The oblique force of my being,
Evicted me from a measured life,
The austere life of perfection.

It thrusted me
Back into the convulsive and uterine world,
Where the animal cry
Bellows at the gate,
Where the engine and the beast
Groan in travail.

In this my certitude,
My sole conviction
Is that my nature does not lie,
That destiny and nature are one.

Clearly my soul's trial,
Its naked ordeal,
Lies in this acceptance:
The reconciliation of what I believe
With the fact of what I am.

This is the wound that tears me apart.
Neither peace of spirit
Nor serenity of soul,
Till that gap closes.

                    *

Why, then, do I fight it?
What is the fester, the seething sore
Refusing to heal?

Pride? That the lofty
Pinnacle of aspiration,
At the eleventh hour of life,
Slipped from my grasp?

Or a morose preoccupation with image,
The disconsolate craving for the high religious profile
The habit of the monk gratuitously confers?

Or mere stubbornness,
A mulish refusal to accept the obvious,
The fact that I failed?

All these and more.
They name the fester;
They do not constitute the wound.

Something seethes beneath them,
More mysterious,
More keen and more blind.

Something lives on that the heart can't help,
Something below the proud flesh of that bruise:
A hunger for God and nothing but God
This world cannot fill.

Neither wife nor child nor fame nor fortune.

The brute thirst for the absolute,
The apotheosis of desire
In the guts of God.

What?
The reconciliation of what I believe
And what I am?

        Rather
Desire slaked in its raw Source.
Intelligence stunned in its Prey.

                *

For in the monastery
What I believed and what I am
Truly *were* one—

Up to a point!

But beyond that point
Something rebelled.

(Not in my spirit:
No real reservation
Troubled my spirit.)

But something more visceral.
Something I can only call
The subsistent self,
The basis of my being.

As a monk
I sought to immolate this subsistent self
In the interest of transcendence
And for years it availed.

But after a time
That basic being climbed down from its cross,
Embracing its need,
Thirstily,
And refused to return.

No matter how I implored.
No matter how I threatened and cajoled.
No matter how I appealed to the supreme imperatives,
The fiery strictures—

(No matter! No matter!)

It would not go back.
It refused to return.

But rather, when the woman came,
It followed her out,
Back to the wild convolutions,
The mouthing and the tonguing,
The bitterness and the dross.

Leaving the spirit stunned.
Leaving the mind sick.
Leaving the soul sullen.

Until, realizing at last
Nothing more could change now,
Nothing save itself alone,
The mind gave over.

In the anguished need for unification
The malleable mind
Relinquished and succumbed.

And now *it* endures crucifixion,
It endures torment and incertitude.

For the spirit's belief,
The soul's conviction,
Lie back in the cell.

*

Somewhere there exists
The crystal prism,
The clear point of reconciliation,
This I know.

To find it is my challenge.

But its shape remains shut,
Closed against the surging myth of futurity,
In the legend of the past—

The dark, blood-ooze origin of things,
The spurt of birth.
And that, after all, is the gasp of completion.

Let then my basic being,
That savageness of soul,
Project the guerdon of its need.

Then my cross-stretched mind
Will grope the deliverance
This flesh could not abide.

THE SCOUT

Passing a leathercraft shop in Mill Valley I see
Yellow buckskin, long undulant fringes,
Lazy-stitch beadwork of the Plains tribes,
Strong, tawny wear of the old frontier.

Buckskin right now is a youthful fad, but not
This grade of the authentic. And turning inside,
On the moment's crystalline decisiveness,
I allow myself to be fitted. The cost:
A hundred dollars down, a hundred
Dollars on delivery. I pay
Without a quiver. Returned home,
I muse by the fire, smoking,
The first of a few slow nights reflection
Before the garb is my own.

                        For the implications
Are revolutionary. Tonight, back in the monastery,
My black and white habit is worn by another.
But now, in the shimmering imagination,
I assume the regalia of the Old West:
Beads, buckskin and bearclaws, the extravagant
Fantastic image. Yet for all the grandiose
Self-projection, which time must erase to confirm,
I know I have come to a steep divide,
A fork in the crooked trail of my life;
That I have truly chosen; will bear that choice;
Wear it about my being, as I learned to bear it,
As I learned to wear it over long years,
In the habit of the monk.

             For a way opens up
Taking me instinctively back,
Back beyond the first frontier, beyond the advent
Of agriculture or the civilized dream,
Back to the Stone Age myth and the ethos of blood.
These rare integuments are its powerful insignia,
A way of ordering what, to the imagination,
Is truly there but rationally denied, and hence
Vague, without substance, lacking essential symbolic force—
Back beyond the confirming vineyard of my youth,
That took me out of my father's world, setting me free—
Back to the archaic mysteries,
The fertility of the soil, the magic of animals,
The power-vision in solitude, the terrifying
Initiation and rebirth, the love
And ecstasy of the dance, modalities
Governing the deeps of instinct,
The seat of consciousness itself,
Where the poet, as shaman to his time,
Ritualizes for the race—all, all subsumed
In the skin of the bison and the antler of the elk,
And borne on the being. Just so
The habit of the monk, received in solemn investiture,
Confirms its tangible ethos, feeds
Participation to the flesh, yields
The meaning it denotes.

             Or so in my musing.
But suddenly a mounted figure rises in my mind,
Abruptly accosting. The single
Eagle feather of the scout marks him Protector,
Watcher of the Spirit, Guardian of the Sacred Mysteries,
Keeper of the Pass.

I raise my hand,
Palm forward, the immemorial gesture of peace.
But wheeling his pony he disappears.
I am left apprehensive, touched by a strange foreboding,
Vaguely disturbed.

Gazing into the flame-lick
I catch for the first time the vibration of menace.
I smell danger at the divide.

THE BLACK HILLS

Riding a horse up a narrow gorge I pick
Traces of an old trail. In my dream
All is weed-grown, brush-choked, my clothes
Tear on quick spines, and here and there
Thorns have scratched blood. Suddenly in the abrupt dusk
My horse spooks and whinnies, refusing to go on.
I dismount and drag forward, exasperated, the bridle
Straining in my left fist as I shoulder through,
Press on and in to a lost clearing.
Then I see, obliquely up-slope, skewed in stark branches,
The ancient tree-burials of the Indians.
This is the place. I have reached at last
My dark quest's end.

                    For it was here,
At the close of the final bloodily-doomed campaign,
A band of exhausted Sioux, burying their dead,
Endured ambush. United States cavalry,
Charging down-slope at dawn, leveled
The ritual-keeping remnant. Braves, squaws,
Even the cradleboard papoose—all alike
Riddled under the skirl of lead
From the snout carbines. Scalped, mutilated,
The sex of the women hacked out with bowie knives,
Jabbed over saddlehorns, to be worn
Swaggering back to the stockade saloons,
Derisive pubic scalps, obscene trophies
Of a decimated people, a scalped land.

Left here the bodies
Made whitened skeletons under the tree-hung graves.
Then blizzard and grizzly scattered about the little clearing
The buzzard-picked bones. With the next spring thaw
Dispersed remnants of other bands found their way here,

52831

Collected the littered remains, grouping them into
    awkward bundles,
Pathetic attempts to reshape the dead,
And hoisted them skyward, joining the earlier
High tree-burials the Plains Indians use on the vast prairies
When the earth is frozen, and now, strange transplants,
Adapted here in the shortness of time
To the dark mountains, the dense firs.

The dust of battle is all washed away with the years.
But the sky-hung mummies still survive the snows.
I see their tattered shrouds
Flutter in the night-wakened wind
That prowls down the canyon.

But my terrified horse balks unmanageably.
Contorted at the clearing's edge he plunges and shrieks.
Thinking it no more than the spectral graves
Terrorizing the acute nostrils and the fearful animal sight,
I tether him short and grope forward alone.
But suddenly the intangible presence tormenting him
Transfixes me. Nailed to the spot
Terror like an electric vibration rivets my being.
Confused, immobilized, fighting to retain consciousness,
I sense the ominous locus, the magnetic spot
From which all that threatens
Issues toward me.

It pours from a spill of shattered boulders
Just beneath the sky-swung graves.
Here the last braves took refuge,
Fought till every arrow was gone,
Fought till the white man's
Pitifully malappropriate firearms
Fell silent in their hands,
Fought with knives arced and the tomahawks
Screaming like insane eagles,

Hacking and whirling over the melee
When the cavalrymen charged in,
Blasting, kicking, gouging,
The pistols spitting till the last riddled body
Jerked limp and flopped dead.

Gazing toward the cluster of rocks
I gather into focus the incredible emanation,
The torrent of hatred pouring into me.
It is as archaic and irreducible as weightless stone,
A kind of psychic lava,
Pouring across the narrow space
And the cavity of the years.

And it is male.
The savage violence.
The primal pride.

For this have I come.

And seeking to master it, to neutralize
The hate, convert
Power to purpose in the need that brought me here,
I project in my imagination the sublime
Patriarchal image I reverenced as a boy,
The composite visage of all the great chiefs,
Their names and singularities: Roman Nose, Black Kettle,
Red Cloud, Crazy Horse, Gall, Sitting Bull . . .
Confronting the torrent of malediction
I wring that image from my buried past,
And give it life.

But the vision fades.
The white man's guilt, founded in my heart,
Warps between, a massive, misshapen block.

I see only the piebald ponies,
Retreating, their tails
Flattened before the blizzard of time,
Humpbacked under the weight of the years,
A splendor despoiled, a ravished pride.

"Father," I cry, "Come back to us!
Return to our lives!"
My words ring through the dusk,
And a wind springs up, rattling the leaves.
"I have come to close the wound,
Heal the gash that cuts us from you,
And hence from the earth!"
I pause, listening intently,
Aware of the unanswering gloom, the dusk
Muffled and intense.
"I have come to bury the hatchet,
That we who must live
May live in peace!"

Something moves there in response,
Of this I feel sure,
But no light remains to let it be seen.
Only, from the heap of rocks,
Like an answering hail of arrows,
The torrent of hate.

I sink to my knees shouting:
"Give me your blessing!"
There is rain in the air now
And no time to lose.
I expose my lacerated hands,
The ancient sign that suffering proves one true.
Leaning into the blast of repudiation
I sway desperately, a lost scout
Swaying on the frozen prairie,
In the killing cold.

Aware only of the unrelenting force
Pouring over and around and through me
I lift my head as the night closes down
And shout the one thing left,
The old, hopeless human attestation:
"I love you!"

The force of malediction
Increases to something almost physical.
And indeed the actual wind,
Pouring down the canyon,
Rises to a roar, bearing a volley of torn leaves,
Twigs, loose bark, flung gravel.

And suddenly the rain begins.

Crouched in the weeds
I summon up again the vision of the chiefs,
Call them back in consciousness:
The painted shields and the war ponies,
The painted bodies and eyes,
Buffalo hats, the lynx-skin headdresses,
An eagle feather dangling for every slain foe;
Rippling war-bonnets trailing to the heels,
The jewel-work of beads and the delicate
Fancy-stitch of porcupine quills, arrow quivers
Furred with the magic skin of the otter—
For an instant I possess it again,
The fabulous, unspeakable vision,
Primitive and elegant,
The unquenchable glory of primal man.

Then it fades. A sudden
Spasm of hysteria doubles me up.
I relapse into uncontrollable sobbing.
"I love you," I scream. "Can't you hear me?
God damn it, I love you!"

*

I wake up shouting. I am in my own bed,
Rigid beside my young wife.
It is hours before dawn.
I rise wordlessly, without making a light.
Shaken and trembling, I grope my way to the adjoining room.
On the grate a few coals
Gleam in the fireplace,
Remnants of last evening's blaze,
Dying in ash. A flood of moonlight
Pours through the window. Standing naked in the dark
I let the feeble warmth of the embers
Caress my cold shins.
I gaze shudderingly into the darkness,
Still plunged in the awful atmospherics of the dream.
Moonlight glows on an improvised mandala
I have fashioned out of my mute desire
And hung in the room:
Two gigantic eagle claws
Fixed above the black and white
Pony-tail braid-ends of the Flathead tribe,
Pinned on a Navajo saddle blanket
And nailed to the wall.
The claws clutch upward. I placed them so,
Following the ghostly eagle's death-flight,
Which left life behind and flew at the sun, its father,
Flew till the great unreal talons
Took peace for prey,
Exultantly, their death beyond death,
Stooped upward, and struck
Peace like a white fawn
In a dell of fire.

I believe it. And believing as well
That what we wear and how we wear it
Bodies forth our hope, the deep implication of our
    underlying need,

I turn to the adjacent wall where, flanking the eagle-claw
    mandala,
My great buckskin coat hangs in the moonlight.
I have placed it high on the wall,
As my religious habit, hung high on the door of the
    monastic cell,
Stood sentinel there
Against the intrusion of the world.
New and untried, like a novice's tunic,
The close-fringed coat yet typifies a faith, the image
Of all I seek to recover in my urgency of quest.

But now, in the aftermath of the dream,
The bravery of buckskin jeers me derisively.
Even as I gaze the Navajo saddle blanket
Glows with the pallor of death,
Some tattered burial wrapping
Salvaged from my dream.

Out on the dunes
The sea falls conclusively,
A muffled, explosive gasp,
Final as doom.

But opening the door
The drench of moonlight embraces me,
A sudden inundation of suffused radiance.
It is the beautiful, unsullied present,
Eternally renewed, eternally reborn.
And it envelops me, and blesses me.
I look up into its immensity and its love,
Its past-dispelling love.
And standing there in the doorway,
All Indian at last,
I lift up my arms and pray.

*

But it is too much—
Too heartbreakingly much.
Shivering I turn back to bed.
The ghost of what was,
All that never again can be,
Bodiless and fleshless,
Gleams in the eagle claws,
A spectral presence as I pass by.

Suddenly I jump like a man stabbed.
Under my feet something cracks sickeningly and collapses.
It is only a plastic toy,
The dropped plaything of my wife's infant child.
But reaching down I feel blood on my thumb,
Where the bones of all the buffalo
Gashed my heel.

THE DUNES

I dream once more: a vision
Sharp, brief and conclusive.

Shipwrecked on a desolate coast
I crouch on the beach,
Miles of interminable dunes behind me,
And watch the rolling, endlessly revolving sea,
That falls incessantly on the rustling sand.
Fog swaddles all. Like a gaunt
Sea-pelican come here to die
I stare before me, hollow-eyed,
Unable to cope with the cold
Sunlessness of the air,
Oppressed by the sand, the stifling
Heavy-hanging fog, the sullen
And indifferent sea.

                    Suddenly from the dunes
Thrills the twitter of a bird.
It pierces the fog like an electric stinger.
It is the call of a woman.
Urgent, imperative, insistent,
It energizes my blood.

And lifting my head
I see that everything has changed.
The world of the possible
Tingles about me, crisp and vivid,
Compelled into being by the sheer
Imperation of a song.

                    Getting to my feet
I follow stiffly where it leads,
Unmindful of fatigue, the call
Echoing as it withdraws, haunting
The beachhead, beckoning
Through the vales of the distant
Strangely inviting dunes.

DARK WATERS

Chipmunk: slash with quick teeth
These rawhide ropes.

Little fox, sleek cat of the thicket,
Puma, ringtail in the quaking bush,
Mink in the meadow.

Weasel-woman:
Drive devils out of my blood.
Scare off fear.

I have made a long run.
I have swum dark waters.

I have followed you through hanging traps.
I have risked it all.

O cut my thongs!

At the fork of your flesh
Our two trails come together.

At your body's bench
I take meat.

NOTE

The lines of verse by Robinson Jeffers quoted in the Preface are from "Love the Wild Swan"; and the ghostly eagle's death flight, from *Cawdor* by the same poet, has been incorporated into "The Black Hills." The vision of the chiefs in that poem is adapted from William Brandon's *The American Heritage Book of Indians;* the astrological quotation in "A Time to Mourn" is from *The Guide to Horoscope Interpretation* by Marc Edmund Jones; and the archaic mysteries in "The Scout" are from a statement by Gary Snyder.

INDEX OF TITLES AND FIRST LINES
(Parts of sequences are indicated by asterisks)

79